GREAT LENT FOR TEENS

GREAT LENT FOR TEENS

by

Arsanie Sawiers

ST SHENOUDA'S MONASTERY
SYDNEY, AUSTRALIA
2017

Great Lent for Teens

ST SHENOUDA MONASTERY
8419 Putty Rd,
Putty, NSW, 2330

www.stshenoudamonastery.org.au

ISBN 13: 978-0-9945710-4-5

About the Author:

Arsanie Sawiers has recently completed a Bachelor of Science (psychology) at Macquarie University. He attends St Sidhom Bishay Coptic Church, Dural, where he serves the high school youth. He also actively participates in various church services.

Cover Design:
Mariana Hanna
In and Out Creation Pty Ltd
inandoutcreations.com.au

Text Layout:
Hani Ghaly,
Begoury Graphics
begourygraphics@gmail.com

Contents

INTRODUCTION

It is a well known fact that all Orthodox, if not all Christian denominations, commonly refer to the Great Lent as "the holiest part of the year." It is considered to be the most vital fasting period in the Orthodox calendar since our Lord Jesus Christ Himself fasted this period.

Before we can begin an investigation into the significance of the Lent period, it is important that we understand why the length of the fast is fifty-five days. The first seven days are termed "Preparation Week." This period is followed by The Holy Forty Days; Lazarus Saturday and finally the "Passover" week (commonly referred to as "Pascha" or "Passion" week). Each of these blocks come together to form the entire period of The Great Lent which will be explored in more depth throughout this book.

In order to completely understand the significance of this event, we will look at how seriously the Original Church Fathers took this period of fasting. Canon 69 from the Canons of our Fathers the Apostles states that "any bishop, priest, deacon, sub-deacon, reader, or psalmist, who does not fast the Holy Forty Days and the fasts of Wednesdays and Fridays is prohibited from performing any service in the Church and partaking of the Holy Communion until he has fasted and received an absolution. As for laymen, they are also prevented from partaking of the Holy Communion until they have once again fasted and received the absolution."

It is crazy to think that for things we as modern-day Christians consider to be completely normal (such as skipping the occasional Wednesday fast), our forefathers would have been excommunicated from the Church or banned from Holy Communion. We refer back to these original Canons not to become afraid of what might happen if we do not practice fasting diligently, but instead so that we might try to understand just why the Church has placed such large emphasis on this period.

The Great Lent is divided into seven weeks, each commencing with a significant event on Sunday. The Church has selected these Sunday readings specifically so that we might benefit on our journey through the fifty-five day period of fasting, giving us strength and reassurance when we need it most. Each week holds a significant event in the life of Christ from which we can extract meaning and apply a practical message to our own lives. This book will be divided into seven chapters, one for each week, and will contain some "Ask Yourself" segments where you are encouraged to stop and reflect on your own life, thinking about how you might be able to apply this lesson as you go about your day-to-day activities.

PREP SUNDAY

LEARN TO PRAY (MATTHEW 6: 1-18)

"But you, when you pray, go into your room, and when you have shut your door, pray to your Father who is in the secret place; and your Father who sees in secret will reward you openly." Matthew 6:6 (NKJV)

LEARN TO PRAY

On the Sunday where we are to begin our preparation for the period of The Great Lent, the Church has selected a very specific reading from the gospel of St. Matthew. It is no coincidence that our forefathers selected this particular passage, perhaps in their wisdom, to place emphasis on the value of effective prayer, encouraging the congregation to learn how to communicate with the Creator.

You will notice that this passage of the Bible can be clearly divided into three sections. The first section, which consists of verses 1-4, talks openly about "giving to the poor" or the wider category of charity.

"Take heed that you do not do your charitable deeds before men, to be seen by them. Otherwise you have no reward from your Father in heaven." (Matthew 1:1 NKJV)

It is important that we understand the significance of this Biblical passage and interpret the message of Christ correctly. For many teenagers and young adults, beginning our Lent journey with a verse such as this one can be disheartening as often we feel that we do not have much to give. Particularly as a teenager, it is unlikely that you will be making enough (if any) money independently, thus giving money to the poor is quite a difficult and indeed a sometimes impossible task.

However, if you read this section carefully, you will notice that there is not a single mention of money as the method by which we should perform our acts of charity. Giving money is most certainly a type of charity, however it is not the only type of charity. Christ uses a much deeper term as He says "charitable deeds." This is great news for those of us who are broke! Christ does not expect you to give the things you do not have. What He does however expect is for you to be charitable with the gifts with which He has blessed you. These things include time, health, service, support and, above all, love. No matter how scarce you may feel your resources are, even if you are in poor health, one thing we, as Christians, cannot argue is that we have no gift with which to be charitable. We who have been baptised have received the Holy Spirit and God has come and dwelt within us, therefore, as God is Love, Love also dwells within us.

If you can be charitable with nothing else, be charitable with the Love of God by which you have been blessed.

The second portion of the passage speaks about how we should communicate with our Heavenly Father. In this portion, Christ teaches those around Him when to pray, how to pray and what to pray about. Saying the "Our Father" has become a habit and repetition for most of us in our lives, which is incredibly ironic as the verse immediately before it states, "do not use vain repetitions." Over the coming seven weeks, we will aim to change this prayer from a repetition to a channel for meditation, beginning today, where we will take apart the Our Father and try to understand the deeper meaning behind each line.

WHEN TO PRAY?

You will notice that this passage tells us to shut our doors and pray secretly in our rooms. This is an incredibile part of our day where we should dedicate some time to spend quietly with God, a lesson which I am sure has been given by parents, servants, priests and maybe even friends. Today, challenge yourself to commit to doing this twice a day, once in the morning and once in the evening, where you spend time with Christ in your room quietly without interruptions or distractions.

However, this is not the only time when you should pray, particularly during this Lent period. In fact, prayer should be an ongoing conversation between you and your Heavenly

People, Places & Things

Forty Days

Forty days recalls various periods of preparation in the Old Testament, including the forty days Moses spent fasting and with God on Mt. Zion at the giving of the Law (Ex. 34:28), the forty days the Israelites spent spying out the Promised Land (Num. 13:25), and the forty years that the Israelites spent wandering in the wilderness before entering the Promised Land (Num. 14:34).

Father as you go about your day. Whilst formal prayer happens in the peace of your room, informal prayer should be happening throughout each activity. Perhaps even only a few words or a sentence or two with God consistently, every hour, every day, has the power to transform your life.

HOW TO PRAY?

We have already mentioned that Christ is very clear in saying that we are not to use "vain repetitions" which means praying aimlessly in order to tick the box saying that we have prayed or to make ourselves feel good. In fact, doing so can be dangerous as it causes the deep words of prayer to lose their meaning as we brush over them carelessly. When we pray, we should pray slowly and in secret, ensuring we think carefully about what we say to God, and reflect even more carefully on what God says to us through the Holy Bible.

WHAT TO PRAY?

Our primary objective for this week is not to attain an incredible gift where we pray the entire Agpeya each night or spend hours weeping on our beds because of our sins. Doing this would be incredible, but if we are being honest, most of us aren't quite "there" yet. Instead, the task this week is simple: Understand what the "Our Father" is intended for and to say it having made sure that we address all the components in our prior prayer.

What the Fathers Say

"Then, let us not make our prayer by the gesture of your body, nor by the loudness of our voice but by the earnestness of our mind"

\- St John Chrysostom

Our Father in heaven,

Hallowed be Your name

This portion of the prayer suggests that we should always begin our prayer by giving praise to God ("Hallowed be Your name") and acknowledging His role in our lives as a Father.

Your kingdom come

Your will be done

On earth as it is in heaven

Here we declare the all-knowing, or omniscient power of God. It is crucial that before saying a line such as this in prayer, you have actually submitted yourself and your life to Christ. If you truly wish for your life here on Earth to be peaceful, glorious and perfect "as it is in Heaven" then you must invite the Prince of Peace to take charge of your life. Kneel before Christ in prayer and humbly acknowledge that you have too much left to learn to try and navigate through life by yourself.

Give us this day our daily bread.

By asking the Lord to give us this day our daily bread, we ask the Lord to provide for us what we need this day. In saying this, we also promise to be content and satisfied with whatever it is God has considered appropriate to be our "daily bread." This means we should not stand before Christ and complain because there is something we want that we do not

What the Fathers Say

"Do you want your prayer to rise upward to the heavens? Provide it, then, with two wings: fasting and alms giving"

– St Augustine

have ("Your will be done", remember!) Let us also remember that God only gives us what we can handle and so if we submit to Him, we do not need to worry about yesterday or tomorrow, only today.

And forgive us our trespasses

As we forgive those who trespass against us

As we reach the final stages of the prayer, we encounter what is perhaps the most difficult part of the process. When praying this sentence, I am directly asking God to forgive me of an entire multitude of sins that I have committed over the span of my life. But there's a catch. Directly tied to that request comes a promise where I look God directly in the eye and say "I have forgiven those who have wronged me." Before praying the Our Father it is important that you acknowledge your own sin with a repentant heart but equally as important that you both acknowledge and dismiss the wrongdoings of others. This is not always easy so think carefully about who you have and have not forgiven before you ask God to "forgive us our trespasses."

And do not lead us into temptation,

But deliver us from the evil one.

Through Jesus Christ our Lord

For Yours is the kingdom and the power and the glory forever. Amen

Before concluding your prayer of the Our Father, ensure that you have noted your weaknesses in the face of sin and temptation, asking that Christ be with you, strengthen you and deliver you from Satan and all his tricks. Finish by acknowledging the power and glory of Christ, asking that one day you be joined to Him in the Kingdom of Heaven. Finally, Christ mentions the importance of fasting. To conclude the Bible Passage as well as this chapter, we will openly admit that fasting is not easy. Fasting is, however, essential. It gives the individual discipline and control over his own body, allowing him greater focus in prayer and giving the strength to overcome sins. This is only successful if the fast is performed earnestly and eagerly without complaining or bragging.

FIRST SUNDAY

SURRENDER (MATTHEW 6: 24-34)

"Therefore I say to you, do not worry about your life, what you will eat or what or what you will drink; nor about your body, what you will put on. Is not life more than food and the body more than clothing?"

– Matthew 6:25 (NKJV)

The Gospel of the first Sunday of the Great Lent acts as a passage of acknowledgement and reassurance for us not only as Christians but also as humans. This week, the Church has selected a specific part of the book of St. Matthew where Christ notes our weaknesses and rebukes our way of thinking. Having already fasted and prayed for seven days during the week of preparation, it is not uncommon that one who has not fasted and prayed regularly in the past begins to feel a very real struggle not only with sin and temptation, but within themselves. Being separated from the foods we love and indeed from our own comfortable routines and forcing ourselves to reflect and contemplate as we begin this journey can be a daunting and difficult task. It is for this reason that the church is incredibly selective, choosing this passage as a means by which to encourage those of us who feel that we are beginning to struggle. Often, it is enough for a person to feel that a difficulty is being acknowledged and normalised in order for them to gain the strength and reassurance to overcome it. In the Bible reading for the first Sunday of the

Great Lent, Christ does just that. The way Christ begins His passage here can sometimes seem a bit harsh. He states very sternly and simply:

"No one can serve two masters; for either he will hate the one and love the other, or else he will be loyal to the one and despise the other. You cannot serve God and mammon."

How can we, as 21st century young Christians, be told that to love possessions or wordly things is to hate God? We have always been taught that the worship of material things distances us from Christ, but we certainly need money and other possessions in order to survive! Besides, who does not love to hear about the latest movies that have been released? Who of us wants to be lacking any of the latest technology? Now whilst Christ is very definitive in that he who is loyal to wealth, or in the case of young people, we can use the word materialism instead, cannot be loyal to God, He does not imply that these things are evil in any way. In fact, when we examine the true definition of the word "mammon" which Christ uses in this passage, we find that it pertains more to the

What the Fathers Say

"Possess, but don't be possessed. Take, but don't be taken. Be a master of your money, and not a slave of it"

- St. Augustine

evil influence or idolatry of material things. So, whilst wanting to live comfortably and always hold the latest iPhone or wear the latest fashion is a completely normal and indeed quite reasonable desire, we need to tread carefully lest we begin to focus more on them than on God. Whilst this might seem to be an unclear and subjective idea, Christ's next words show us quite easily how to distinguish between a harmless desire for comfort and a dangerous passion for Worldly things.

"Therefore I say to you, do not worry about your life, what you will eat or what you will drink; nor about your body, what you will put on. Is not life more than food and the body more than clothing? Look at the birds of the air, for they neither sow nor reap nor gather into barns; yet your heavenly Father feeds them. Are you not of more value than they? (Matthew 6:25-26 NKJV)

The way to debunk this controversial matter is simple. Am I constantly thinking about my desires, including food? Do I find myself bothered when I can't have the latest technological or fashion trends? If the answer to any of these is yes, then it is possible you

People, Places &Things

Money

Money in itself is not a sin. But on the contrary, money is a blessing and a good gift. All the danger that is generated is from the love of money. The love of money is the origin of all evil. The love of money destroys faith. It cancels the dependence on God and affects the worship within its core. No one could worship two masters, God and money.

may be more attached to your material things than you should be.

Christ goes on to revoke these obsessions and stresses by reminding the congregation that things are not actually always in our power. For us, I think the verse in Matthew 6:27 serves as a call for us to humble ourselves in the face of the Lord. Sure, life can be stressful, particularly as you get older and there are bills to pay, things to buy, activities to do and people to care for. However just after, Christ reminds us that our Heavenly Father will be taking care of our needs just as He does the birds in Heaven, He starkly reminds us that worrying doesn't do any good.

"Which of you by worrying can add one cubit to his stature?" (Matthew 6:27 NKJV)

So, this week we are called to surrender ourselves to God. Christ wants us to turn our lives over to Him as we progress through this journey. He acknowledges that we have our concerns and stresses and that we are weak in our humanity, but He also states that it has all already been taken care of by your Heavenly Father.

What the Fathers Say

"What good is it if we abstain from eating birds and fish, but bite and devour our brothers?"

– St. John Chrysostom

Mammon

The word "mammon" is mentioned in the Bible four times, and three of those times Jesus said it. But what does it mean? The word mammon comes from the Greek word mammonas. Similar root words exist in Hebrew, Latin, Aramaic, Chaldean and Syriac. They all translate to "money, riches, and material possessions."

What the Fathers Say

"Fasting of the body is to cease from food and drink. Yet, the spiritual fasting means that man should be hungry and thirsty for righteousness"

- St. John El-Tabayssi

The conclusion of this week's Biblical passage is one that should be focused on as Christ no longer makes suggestions or statements, but rather, He gives both a command and a promise:

"Therefore do not worry, saying, 'What shall we eat?' or 'What shall we drink?' or 'What shall we wear?' But seek first the kingdom of God and His righteousness, and all these things shall be added to you." (Matthew 6: 31, 33).

When we think about our Father in Heaven and reflect on all the grace bestowed upon us, it is almost offensive for us to become preoccupied with materialism and wealth. When we obsess over fashion trends, cars, technology or anything superficial of this world, it is almost as if we say to Christ that we don't trust Him to provide for us what we need. Instead, we begin to depend on our own wisdom and strength to provide for ourselves. Christ promises that when we turn our attention to Him before all these things, all our desires will be added as a bonus. In saying that though, when your attention is truly focused on Christ, the things of the world cease to matter. How else would it make any sense for a person such as St. Anthony the Great to leave behind the world and live in a cave away from society? The answer is simple! His attention was so focused on God that society and all it's claimed "benefits" weren't worth anything to him anymore.

Finally, Christ is clear that just because we have trust in God it does not mean that we are to omit responsibility from ourselves.

Just as in the story of Joseph while he was in Egypt and worked incredibly hard in order to become the King's Advisor, so too do we need to work if we wish to prosper. So work hard, but when the work's day is done and you've done what you need to do, turn it over to God.

"Therefore do not worry about tomorrow, for tomorrow will worry about its own things. Sufficient for the day is its own trouble." (Matthew 6:34 NKJV)

WHAT IS WEALTH ANYWAY

Once upon a time, there lived a very rich and wealthy man in a big town. He led a luxurious life. He always boasted about his wealth to his friends and relatives.

His son was studying in a distant city and he returned home for vacation. The rich man wanted to show off to his son how rich he was. But his son wasn't fond of any luxurious lifestyle. However, the rich man wanted to make his son realise that his lifestyle was extremely rich and that poor people suffered a lot. He planned a day's visit to the entire town to show him the life of the poor people.

The father and the son took a chariot and visited the entire town. They returned home after two days. The father was happy that his son was very quiet after seeing the poor people honouring the rich man and after witnessing the sufferings of the poor due to lack of facilities.

The rich man asked his son, "Dear son, how was the trip? Did you enjoy it?"

"Yes dad, it was a great trip with you," the son replied.

"So, what did you learn from the trip?" the father asked.

The son was silent.

"Finally you have realised how the poor suffer and how they actually live," said the father.

"No father," replied the son. He added, "We have only two dogs, they have 10 dogs. We have a big pool in our garden, but they have a massive bay without any end! We have luxurious and expensive lights imported from various countries, but they have countless stars lighting their nights. We have a house on a small piece of land, but they have abundant fields that go beyond the horizon. We are protected by huge and strong walls around our property, but they bond with each other and surround themselves with their fellow beings. We have to buy food from them, but they are so rich that they can cultivate their own food." The rich father was stunned and speechless, on hearing his son's words.

Finally the son added, "Dad, thank you so much for showing me who is rich and who is poor. Thank you for letting me understand how poor we really are!"

SECOND SUNDAY

Events

TEMPTATION

TEMPTATION (MATTHEW 4:1-10)

"But He answered and said, "It is written, 'Man shall not live by bread alone, but by every word that proceeds from the mouth of God.'"

- *Matthew 4:4 NKJV*

The second Sunday of the Great Lent tells a story that every single one of us can relate to where Christ truly leads by example, knowing full well the struggles we encounter in our weakness. This week the Church has selected the passage from the Gospel where Christ is tempted on the mountain by Satan.

"Then Jesus was led up by the Spirit into the wilderness to be tempted by the devil. And when He had fasted forty days and forty nights, afterward He was hungry." (Matthew 4: 1-2 NKJV)

Perhaps one of the most astounding factors in the opening of this story that many people might question is how could God be hungry? But Christ made Himself weak as an example, He did not need to fast but did so to meet us in our most vulnerable state. He desired to show us what we could expect when we are at points of weakness. By meeting us at our weakest state, He shares with us in our hardships and in our victories too.

You should note that during this time Jesus' fast was not the same as today, but rather a complete abstinence of food and drink. Such an idea seems crazy but trying to imitate the sacrifice of Christ is perhaps one of the most beneficial spiritual practices for a modern day Christian. In a society where everything is convenient and available at the swipe of a phone or click of a button,

being able to show enough self-control to deny yourself one meal a day in the morning or evening has immense benefit for one's discipline and spiritual life. Now is a perfect time to try and create some distance from your social media. As well as food, cut back the amount of time you spend on your phones, computers and consoles as abstaining from these distractions can be just as beneficial for your spiritual life as abstaining from food.

"Now when the tempter came to Him, he said, "If You are the Son of God, command that these stones become bread." But He answered and said, "It is written, 'Man shall not live by bread alone, but by every word that proceeds from the mouth of God."

(Matthew 4: 3-4 NKJV)

The importance of fasting is that it allows us to follow in the footsteps of Christ. In following His footsteps, we also partake in His victory! A verse we often quote is "Man shall not live by bread alone but by every word that proceeds from the mouth of God." However, did you know that Christ was actually quoting Scripture when he presented this rebuttal to Satan's temptation? The original verse actually appears in the book of Deuteronomy 8:3 and so, by reciting the verse Christ actually emphasised the importance of the Word of God!

But how can you be satisfied and content with the word of God if you don't know it? How can you expect to fight the temptations

What the Fathers Say

"Our leader, Jesus, permitted the temptation for Himself just to teach His children how they can fight"

- St. Augustine

of Satan using faith in Christ's message if you have never studied or contemplated on what that message actually is?

Christ is particularly adamant in making clear the importance of knowing and being able to recite the Scripture as He uses it as a shield by which to overcome temptation more than once in this passage. Practically, it would be unreasonable to expect yourself to memorise all the scripture in one week; one period of Lent, one year or even one lifetime! In fact, many spend an entire lifetime committed to understanding the Word of God when the fact of the matter is, the closer you come to Christ the more you understand and interpret from His Word. Part of the beauty of Biblical reading is that something you might read today may bear an entirely different relevance to what it will have for you if you had read it two years ago. The same will apply two years from now. After all;

Have you not known? Have you not heard? The everlasting God, the Lord, The Creator of the ends of the earth, Neither faints nor is weary. His understanding is unsearchable. (Isaiah 40:28 NKJV)

While it would be naïve to say that we would ever fully understand everything in

People, Places &Things

Wilderness:

When Jesus was tempted He was not in a city or a town, but in the wilderness. The devil attacks most often when he sees men left alone and by themselves. He also did this in the beginning with Eve, after finding her alone and apart from her husband. Therefore, because of this, we greatly need to always be together, so that we may not be open to the devil's attacks

the Bible and every word of God, it would be equally as naïve not to make every effort. When we pray, we are talking to God, when we read the Bible, we are listening to His response. A practical application in our lives would be to try to memorise Biblical passages. . Often, the idea of memorisation is looked on negatively, as though there's no benefit to simply learning His words. But the beautiful thing about filling our minds with the word of the Bible is that when you speak, you will find that you begin to speak the words you've learnt. What a fantastic thing that would be not only for ourselves, but for all those around us too!

Most people have a few really close friends in their lives. Some would even say that they have one stand-out "best friend." The thing you will notice with best friends is that they often tend to think the same way or know what the other person is thinking, which is why they often end up at the principal's office after laughing hysterically at something when nobody else knows what's going on. The reason this happens is because they've

What the Fathers Say

This is the cause of all evils, the not knowing of the Scriptures. We go into battle without arms, and how are we to come off safe?"

\- St. John Chrysostom

Temptation:

The Greek word used here for temptation (peirazo) does not indicate that Jesus had the disordered desire that we refer to in English as temptation. Instead, it means "to try," "to attempt." Here the devil tries to get Jesus to sin and fails.

spent so much time together, had so many conversations and have been in so many situations that one can anticipate how the other person would think. In fact, you could say that the two become so close together that they begin to take on qualities of one another.

Our relationship with God works in the exact same way, but only by spending so much time talking and listening, being in situations together and acknowledging each other's company can we ever truly get there. It's hard to miss that there are certain people we meet who seem to have a religious or scriptural explanation for everything that goes on in their lives. They always seem to be quoting something from the Bible or referring back to God in some way. Perhaps this is because they have established such a close connection with Christ that they begin to think, and speak, in the same way He does. What a beautiful thing!

The final component of the passage for this Sunday is a truly incredible thing for us to witness and aspire to. Christ, having been tempted and resisting this temptation by taking comfort in Scripture send Satan away from Himself;

"Then Jesus said to him, "Away with you, Satan! For it is written, 'You shall worship the LORD your God, and Him only you shall serve.'"

(Matthew 4:10 NKJV)

This is the kind of strength that can be achieved through earnest fasting and prayer as we establish ourselves firmly in the Word of God. By establishing a deep and fulfilling personal relationship with our Heavenly Father we automatically begin to become more diligent in the spiritual battles we are faced with.

REFLECTION

How often do we use the Scripture as a means of defense against the temptations of the devil? How many veses do I know by heart?

THIRD SUNDAY

RETURN TO GOD (LUKE 15:11-32)

RETURN TO GOD

The Reading of the Third Sunday of the Great Lent comes from the Gospel of St. Luke and tells the parable of the prodigal son, a symbol for each and every one of us. It is appropriate that the Church makes quite clear the consequences for those who choose to abandon God and live in sin, indulging their own flesh and satisfying their desires. Indeed, he who separates himself from Christ becomes hungry, for as mentioned last week, man shall not live by bread alone.

It can sometimes be quite difficult for us to understand why the Church would choose the time of Great Lent to emphasise this story. Surely, now, having fasted and prayed for a number of weeks, having finally begun to read our Bibles once again, we are closer with God than ever before? This might be true, but the reality is that every single person has strayed away from God in some way and it can be difficult to truly feel the acceptance and love of the Father surrounding you when you are still holding on to guilt or baggage from your previous choices. This story wasn't written to emphasise the departure of the son, but rather, to clearly depict his story of repentance and the forgiveness of the father so that we, too, might feel truly forgiven and accepted when we stand in the presence of the Lord. Ironically, the prodigal son who departed from his father's house in search of fulfilment and joy ended having less and being in a greater state of helplessness than ever before. It is all too often that we, as members of God's family, take what we think is rightfully ours (our talents, gifts and blessings) and begin to try to make our own way away from God. However, this always ends the same way. We, like the prodigal son, feel dissatisfied and discontent when we separate ourselves from God. Think of how many people who have all the power, money and wealth in the World fall into depression. Some of the most well-renowned and most well-loved celebrities have taken their own lives because they, despite having everything here on Earth, cannot satisfy this state of "want."

Luckily for us, Christ speaks a parable whereby we can easily overcome this dilemma and find ourselves both reunited with the Father and content in His love once again.

"But when he came to himself, he said, 'How many of my father's hired servants have *bread enough and to spare, and I perish with hunger!" (Luke 15: 17 NKJV)*

Let us note the phrase "came to himself" before we proceed in reflecting on this verse. Often, when we imagine the idea of repentance and returning to the Father, we picture a person standing before an icon of Christ, candle lit before the icon, tears flowing down the person's face as they have a life-changing moment of forgiveness.

However, while this is a very romantic image for us to imagine, it might not always be the most realistic for each of us. In fact, if you wait for such a moment, it is unlikely

What the Fathers Say

"Sin means death. It is separation from God, and deprivation of Him. It is wondering and loss. Sin is a defeat rather than a triumph"

- H.H. Pope Shenouda III

your repentance will ever truly happen and if it does, it will be such an emotional and spontaneous repentance, that you will likely return to your old ways shortly after. Instead, we must come to ourselves like the prodigal son. To put it another way, we must return to our senses and realise the error of our ways. This can only be achieved through quiet time reflecting on our choices and thoughts and must be done daily if we ever wish to truly live a life of repentance.

The repentant son returned to his father hoping for nothing more than acceptance. Such is our responsibility when we aim to depart from a life of sin and return to God. This week, it is important to "come to yourself" in humility, meditating on your choices each day and praying for absolution from the Father. However, be careful that you do not confuse humility with self-loathing as Satan can often trick a person into thinking they are being humble when really they are distancing themselves from God by focusing on feelings of unworthiness. Until next Sunday, spend some time each night thinking about what choices you might have made that would

What the Fathers Say

"Everyday that you do not sit with yourself and think about the day's sins and your shortcomings and to help yourself up again, then do not count the day as part of your life."

- St. Isaac the Syrian

People, Places &Things

The Ring:

The father gave the son a ring. Wearing rings during this time in history was a sign of both wealth and position. The power of this symbol reflects the father's desire to restore his son as a family member and a respectable member of the community

'Prodigal' Son:

The word "Prodigal" doesn't mean rebellious or lost—it means "wasteful" and "extravagant." The word origin refers to a person who's reckless and squanders their wealth.

be considered similar to walking away from God. Acknowledge these errors, repent, pray and attend confession. Immediately after this take a moment to reflect on the promise of God:

If we confess our sins, He is faithful and just to forgive us our sins and to cleanse us from all unrighteousness." (1 John 1:9 NKJV) The second half of the parable focuses on the qualities of the father more so than the downfalls of the son. The first and perhaps most vital thing to notice is mentioned in verse twenty:

"And he arose and came to his father. But when he was still a great way off, his father saw him and had compassion, and ran and fell on his neck and kissed him." (Luke 15:20 NKJV)

There are two incredible details to notice here about the father in this story. The first is that the father saw his son whilst the son was still a great way off. This would imply that the father was constantly looking for the son and hoping for his return. It is not so hard to imagine as so many parents do this exact

The Father

Therefore instead of corruption, He clothes him with an incorruptible garment; instead of hunger, He kills the fattened calf; instead of far journeys, He watched for his return, providing shoes for his feet; and, what is most wonderful, placed a divine signet ring upon his hand; while by all these things He created him anew according to the image of the glory of Christ. These are the gracious gifts of the Father, by which the Lord honours and nourishes those who abide with Him, and those who return to him and repent.

thing, waiting up for their children to return home if their children are ever late, earnestly seeking their safe return. Our Heavenly Father does exactly this, praying that all his children return to him. The second detail is that the father, when finally embracing his son, does not make reference to his betrayal or his actions but rather focuses primarily on his safe return.

"For this my son was dead and is alive again; he was lost and is found.' And they began to be merry." (Luke 15:24 NKJV)

In this story, the father bestows upon his son a kiss, a robe, a ring, sandals on his feet and a fatted calf for the feast.

"But the father said to his servants, 'Bring out the best robe and put it on him, and put a ring on his hand and sandals on his feet. And bring the fatted calf here and kill it, and let us eat and be merry." (Luke 15:22-23 NKJV)

In this story, the father bestows upon his son a kiss, a robe, a ring, sandals on his feet and a fatted calf for the feast.

"But the father said to his servants, 'Bring out the best robe and put it on him, and put a ring on his hand and sandals on his feet. And bring the fatted calf here and kill it, and let us eat and be merry." (Luke 15:22-23 NKJV)

Rather than dishonouring his son for his decision to abandon him, the father chooses instead to glorify his son for having the courage to return. It can be said that the kiss is a sign of that sacred peace which can exist only with the Heavenly Father. It is undeniable that we are all sinners. To be human by definition is to be imperfect and to have flaws and as such God would not expect you to be perfect. Sometimes it is easy to fall into a train of thought that because of your sins and imperfections you might be unworthy to stand in the presence of God or to partake of Holy Communion. Christ spoke this parable to remove that exact perception, instead noting that the son was forgiven not because of anything to do with him, but simply because of the loving nature of the Father.

All you need to do is take the first steps in returning to God.

REFLECTION

Do we ever fall in despair and doubt God's ability to restore us his beloved children? Be sure that God's grace is sufficient and He is always waiting for your return.

FOURTH SUNDAY

POWER OF THE OUTCAST

THE POWER OF THE OUTCAST (JOHN 4:1-42)

The passage for this week is the story of the Samaritan woman who encountered Christ when drawing water from a well. Whilst the passage is long and quite deep, we will focus primarily on three main components of the story:

1) *The Everlasting Water (John 4:1-15)*

Before exploring the story of Jesus and the Samaritan woman, it is absolutely necessary that we understand the context of the time. Jews were to have no interactions with Samaritans so for Jesus to even reach out and speak to her was not something to be overlooked. Christ operates the same way with the sinner. Whilst it was no coincidence that Jesus was "weary" as God takes every opportunity to pursue those who seek Him, it is even more incredible to think that the glorious and holy Lord, flawless and perfect, brings Himself to the level of a weak and sinful human in order to bring them to eternal life.

After a conversation with the Samaritan woman who resembles all of us the weak and sinful, Christ introduces her to a concept she had never before heard of, living water. What we should admire about the Samaritan woman is her eagerness to learn and embrace this interaction with Christ, a keenness that many of us, even as Christians who already know Him lack.

"The woman said to Him, "Sir, You have nothing to draw with, and the well is deep. Where then do You get that living water? Are You greater than our father Jacob, who gave us the well, and drank from it himself, as well as his sons and his livestock?" (John 4:11-12 NKJV)

Just as Christ states in Matthew 7:7 "Ask and you shall receive, seek and you shall find", He immediately provides the woman with a deeper insight into Himself and she immediately seeks union with Him. Similarly, when we are honest and persistent in prayer, God often makes Himself more known to us having seen an eagerness to establish a deeper relationship with Him.

"Jesus answered and said to her, "Whoever drinks of this water will thirst again, but whoever drinks of the water that I shall give him will never thirst. But the water that I shall give him will become in him a fountain of water springing up into everlasting life. The woman said to Him, "Sir, give me this water, that I may not thirst, nor come here to draw."" (John 4:13-15 NKJV)

People, Places & Things

Jews vs Samaritans:

After the death of Solomon, the twelve tribes split into two separate kingdoms: Judah in the South and Samaria in the North. The northern kings worshipped pagan idols and were always fighting with Jerusalem. This rivalry escalated over time, and therefore the Samaritan woman rightfully said: 'Jews have no dealing with Samaritans'.

2) "I have no husband." (John 4:16-27)

What the Fathers Say

"She had come as a reject. He sent her back being accepted by God Himself. She came wounded. He sent her back whole. She came laden with questions. He sent her back as a source for answers. She came living a life of quiet desperation. She ran back overflowing with hope"

- St. Clement

When the Samaritan woman encounters Christ, she is made more aware of a sin she has tried to cover up. This change is inevitable as you approach Christ, who is the light of the World (see 1 John 1:5), those blemishes and imperfections in yourself which you may have previously overlooked or ignored in the darkness begin to become more visible. What you choose to do with this information is what defines who you become as a Christian.

"Jesus said to her, "Go, call your husband, and come here." The woman answered and said, "I have no husband." Jesus said to her, "You have well said, 'I have no husband,' foryou have had five husbands, and the one whom you now have is not your husband; in that you spoke truly." John 4:16-17 (NKJV)

The Samaritan woman, when told that Christ knows about her adultery, chooses to pursue Him further. It is natural for someone who is made aware of a sin that they have previously tried to cover up to become angry or ashamed, trying desperately to protect their reputation. When you look at the bigger picture, we are all called to Christ because we are imperfect, and the exposure of your hidden sins as you connect with Christ should not push you away, but rather bring you closer to Him. How can you fix something that you cannot see? Just as a doctor would not perform surgery on a patient without clearly seeing what they are working on, likewise, your soul can not be healed until it is brought closer to the light of Christ.

Therefore, there would be no point in trying to hide or cover up those sins that you are most ashamed of. Many young people are so disgusted in themselves for their mistakes, particularly if they struggle with sexual sins or pornography, so much so that they try to hide them from their confession Father. You wouldn't hide a body part that was causing your health to suffer from a doctor, so why would you hide this from your spiritual guide?

3) "Now we believe." (John 4:28-42)

Finally, we have seen the light of Christ. Whilst the process is uncomfortable and can make us feel scared and vulnerable, it was the best possible thing for us because we now feel more connected with Christ than ever before. So what do we do next?

The woman then left her waterpot, went her way into the city, and said to the men, "Come, see a Man who told me all things that I ever did. Could this be the Christ? (John 4:28-29 NKJV)

We, as Christians have a responsibility to introduce the rest of the World to our God. In fact, whilst God is light, Christ also instructs Christians saying that we are "the light of the World." Jesus makes it very clear to his disciples that they must let their light (and their knowledge of the true light) shine before men, giving others the opportunity to encounter Him and experience salvation for themselves.

It is very possible that you might be somebody's only chance at ever meeting Christ. To put it simply: your actions might

What the Fathers Say

"His "drink" was to do the will of him that sent him. That was why he said, "I thirst; give me to drink," namely, to work faith in her and to drink of her faith and transplant her into his own body, for his body is the church"

- St. Augustine

make the difference for someone's salvation.

It's difficult to think about, as somebody who is still struggling with sin. It isn't uncommon to feel weak or unworthy. These are normal feelings. The Samaritan woman had just been told by Christ that He knew about her numerous husbands and her adultery. In fact, she was probably feeling as disgusting and unworthy as any of us ever have. But she decided to spread the light of Christ anyway, because she had experienced what it meant to truly know Him. Verse 42 shows how beautiful the results of overcoming those feelings can be.

Then they said to the woman, "Now we believe, not because of what you said, for we ourselves have heard Him and we know that this is indeed the Christ, the Savior of the world." (John 4:42 NKJV)

Christ manifested Himself to these people, not because of the Samaritan woman, but through her. Had it not been for her own journey that day, meeting with Christ and spreading His light, these people may never have had the opportunity to meet their Saviour.

REFLECTION

Just like the Samaritan woman repented when she admitted her sins to Christ, let's strive to be diligent in our daily repentance and honest in our confession.

FIFTH SUNDAY

HOPE (JOHN 5:1-18)

In the reading for the fifth Sunday of the Great Lent, a man who has been suffering from an illness for a prolonged period of time is healed by Christ. This passage is full of symbols related to the salvation of humanity and therefore provides all Christians with lessons from which we can learn and apply in our own lives.

Perhaps this may seem an abstract concept to us today, a place where every so often an angel stirred in the pool and healed the ailment of the first person to touch the water. It may seem like a strange and even radical concept to imagine but in fact, we have all been healed a number of times in this very same way through the Church. The heavenly angel becomes a symbol for the incarnation of Christ, coming down to heal us from our sin as a Heavenly Physician and the man by the pool resembles us all more frequently than we might realise.

HOPE

An important fact that many people may overlook in the case of this man, who has been sick for thirty-eight years, was the man's own willingness and effort in order for his healing to occur. Last week when reflecting on the Samaritan woman, we highlighted that often Christ seeks out those who are in need of His grace. Similarly, Christ seeks out the sick man by the pool but only because He sees that he has both initiated and sustained an effort to receive this healing. The idea of a man who has been struggling with an illness for such a large number of years and still comes to the pool and seeks healing is ridiculous. For so many of us, how quick are we to give up on God when something in our lives does not go to plan? We throw away our hope in God's plan for us and sometimes even begin to blame Him for our failures when we don't get the test results we wanted, or have a problem in one of our relationships. However, what we see in today's story is the power of trusting in God and the way in which Christ deals with those who do not give up hope in Him.

"When Jesus saw him lying there, and knew that he already had been in that condition a long time, He said to him, "Do you want to be made well?" (John 5:6 NKJV)

The beautiful thing about this question is that Christ does not wait for the request of the sick in order to heal them but rather, He runs to provide comfort and compassion to the one who is in need. When Christ asks the sick man if he wants to be made well it is not because He does not know the desire of the

Pool of Bethesda:

The Pool of Bethesda is Hebrew for "house of mercy". The Sheep Gate was probably so called because the priests used to wash the sacrificial lambs before taking them into the Temple. The pool is a type of Christian baptism in which believers enjoy a new birth and healing of sin. The Angel coming down from heaven typifies the Incarnate Logos of God, the Heavenly Physician.

man, if he didn't want to be made well, why would he have been waiting by the pool in the first place? Instead, Christ asks because He wishes to stir up in the man a greater passion for this healing, indicating that He is willing to give His grace to this man if only he now asks from the Lord.

What the Fathers Say

"As Christ becomes the water of healing, even if you had immersed the whole World into the pool, you would not consume the grace, nor exhaust the gift."

- St. John Chyrsostom

This incredible pool provided healing to anyone who entered it, however, only one person would be healed each time the angel stirred up the water. With Christ, there is no limit to His Grace and healing.

"The sick man answered Him, "Sir, I have no man to put me into the pool when the water is stirred up; but while I am coming, another steps down before me." (John 5:7 NKJV)

The man, who was obviously sick and unable to move as an average person would, instead of becoming angered with Christ or trying to convince Christ to heal him answers so simply. For most of us, if Christ was to say to us "Do you want to be made well from this sin you've struggled with for years?" we would throw our hands in the air and say "Of course I want to be made well! What kind of a ridiculous question is that!?" This man opens his heart to Christ instead of becoming irritated by what seems like a completely illogical question. He communicates with Christ openly and honestly, shares with Him the fact that this illness has tormented him, that he feels he has nobody else to rely on in this struggle, that he has tried a number of times but cannot do it alone.

This week of Lent is a perfect opportunity for us to really bring ourselves closer to the pool of healing and the grace of Christ. We have now been on this journey of Lent for some time and as such are probably starting to feel more than ever before the gift of salvation for which Christ gives up his life on the Cross in a few weeks time. As Christ resurrects and opens the gates of paradise, giving each of us the chance to partake in it, He almost asks us "Do you want to be made well?" Today is a great time for us to begin our struggle against those sins which impact us more than most of the others. The sins people struggle with will vary from person to person but the most common ones include things like engaging in one's sexual desires, gossiping and swearing. If you haven't done so yet in this fasting period, today is the day you must begin to fight against this sin aggressively. This is important so that when the Feast of the Holy Resurrection comes to pass and you are filled with joy for the gift of Salvation you can answer Christ saying that you, like the man by the pool in Bethesda, have struggled as much as you can with the sin and have nobody else to rely on but Christ and His Grace. The paralytic found life not in the old pool, but in the living Christ. Our Lent season also reminds us that this is where we find new life and constant renewal as well.

"Jesus said to him, "Rise, take up your bed and walk." And immediately the man was made well, took up his bed, and walked." (John 5:8-9 NKJV)

Why did Jesus tell the man to rise and walk instead of immediately telling him he was healed? The answer to this question is rather simple. In the case of this man, just as in the case of all our lives, Christ makes it clear that the work is not finished once you have received His grace and are healed. Christ is making an example of this man to suggest that whilst He is the giver of healing and salvation, we too need to be proactive in our healing and not just in our repentance. Suppose the man had said "But how can I walk? You know I have an illness", perhaps he may have never been healed. However, it is only when we have full faith in the power and wisdom of God each time we partake in His divine healing through the Body and Blood of Christ on the altar that we can truly be made well.

In this story Christ also gives a stern warning which seems quite harsh to process.

"Afterward Jesus found him in the temple,

and said to him, "See, you have been made well. Sin no more, lest a worse thing come upon you." (John 5:14 NKJV)

Christ does not often say things like this, as we all know, His nature is loving and compassionate throughout the Bible just as it is with us. Although these words seem almost as though they are a threat, it is much more likely that Christ warns the man against himself. What could be worse than an ailment which made it difficult for him to move all these years? Perhaps with his renewed strength and mobility, the man may find himself more capable of involving himself in sin than before. When Christ was speaking of a "worse thing" He was certainly warning the man about the dangers of a life in condemnation as a result of sin rather than a physical punishment on the Earth. Similarly for us, having undergone repentance and confession we often feel very spiritually graced, just as this man felt more active and mobile. This is a beautiful thing, but we must be diligent and careful not to fall into old habits as it is not uncommon that having experienced this beautiful spirituality and falling back into sin, people begin to feel so ashamed and disgusted with themselves they often end up even worse off than when they started.

What the Fathers Say

"Jesus singled out the man who had waited for 38 years in order to teach us to have perseverance, and as a judgement against those who lose hope or patience in much lesser troubles lasting a far shorter time"

- St John Chrysostom

SIXTH SUNDAY

Events

A REPRESENTATIVE OF CHRIST

A REPRESENTATIVE OF CHRIST (JOHN 9:1-41)

"The man answered and said to them, "Why, this is a marvelous thing, that you do not know where He is from; yet He has opened my eyes!" John 9:30 NKJV

We have now reached the final week of the period of Lent before entering into the Pascha week. Surely it has been a time where many of us have struggled with self-discipline, temptation and the desire to return to old habits but hopefully we've also become more connected with our spiritual lives through the Agpeya, Bible and quiet time in these past weeks. The story of the man who was born blind and received sight is a truly symbolic journey of each person who comes closer to the light of Christ as we have all been doing over the past forty days.

There are all manners of blindness in this Gospel lesson. The man born blind has one form of blindness – a physical blindness, but there are many forms of blindness that inflict humans as the Gospel lesson reveals.

"I must work the works of Him who sent Me while it is day; the night is coming when no one can work. As long as I am in the world, I am the light of the world." (John 9:4-5 NKJV)

Christ here suggests that we, as members in Him, must do the work of God while it is day. He follows this by saying that He is the Light of the World which is to mean that we must do God's work wherever Christ is present – wherever the church or members of

Christ's Body are. This means two things for the modern day Christian; the first is that we have an obligation to partake in some form of service so as to fulfil this commandment and the second is that we should always be surrounded by Christ and our fellow members in Christ. This may mean that we need to separate ourselves from certain people or places that distract us from performing God's work or even from God Himself. Now let us turn our attention to the way by which Christ heals this man:

"When He had said these things, He spat on the ground and made clay with the saliva; and He anointed the eyes of the blind man with the clay. And He said to him, "Go, wash in the pool of Siloam." So he went and washed, and came back seeing." (John 9:6-7 NKJV)

Christ's use of His own saliva mixed with mud indicates that the virtue of healing in every thing belongs to Christ; clay made of Christ's spit is much more precious and powerful than any medication or ointment we could ever imagine.

The Pool of Siloam:

The pool of Siloam was on the outskirts of Jerusalem, a considerable distance from the temple. From this pool, water was taken for the rites connected with the Feast of the Tabernacles. Siloam, translated, Sent, symbolises Christ, the One sent by the Father. The healing of the blind man confirmed Christ's claim to be the light of the world.

People, Places & Things

What the Fathers Say

"This mixture of clay and saliva is a type of the creation of humanity from the earth. Christ reveals His divinity by restoring part of creation using the same material with which He created humanity in the beginning"

– St. Irenaeus

Christ did this to magnify His power in making a blind man see by a method that one would think more likely to make someone blind. Putting clay on the eyes would close them instead of open them but the power of God often works by contraries; and He makes men feel their own blindness before He gives them sight so that they may appreciate when they see. Often in our lives we have periods of spiritual lows where we feel as though we truly cannot see the Light of Christ in our lives. This is completely normal and happens to everybody so don't feel ashamed if this has happened or is happening to you right now! Instead, try to imagine the blind man with clay covering his face as Christ creates eyes for him from the dirt, just as He created man from the dirt, then suddenly, he saw more clearly than ever. This goes back to the creation of Adam from the clay and truly shows the divine nature of Jesus Christ.

The second reason Christ uses this combination of saliva and mud is to represent and highlight the healing and opening of the eyes of the mind by the grace of Jesus Christ. The design of the gospel is to open men's eyes (see Acts 26:18) and just as Christ is the Word that proceeds from the Father and opens our eyes, so too was this mix that Christ made. This reminds us of the Litany of the Gospel which we hear in every mass where the Priest recites, *"Blessed are your eyes for what they see and your ears for what they hear... that we may hear and act according to Your Holy Gospel."*

Russian Orthodox priest Fr. Jonah Campbell contemplates on this chapter, stating that in reality, all men are born blind, like the man in today's Gospel, though this "blindness" is a spiritual blindness rather than a physical one. Each of us finds himself unable to see clearly as a result of the fall of our first parents Adam and Eve. The Fall resulted in a distortion in the powers of man resulting in our spiritual will being made subject to our minds and bodies.

Before Christ's incarnation, each of us was in darkness, unable to see our passions or appreciate the extent of our sin. In the Holy Sacraments of the Church, however, we have all been granted the gift of spiritual sight. Just as in the example from today's Gospel, where the Saviour used clay to heal the eyes of the man blind from birth, the Saviour has ordained the use of apparently ordinary material things to accomplish our healing within the Church: the waters of baptism, the sacred oil of the Mayroun and, of course, the bread and wine that are transformed into the Sacred Body and Blood of Our Lord God and Saviour Jesus Christ.

We must truly bring forth repentance to our Saviour and learn the lesson from the other blind man on the road to Bartimaos and continually call out to our Saviour from the depths of our souls saying, "Jesus, Son of David, have mercy on me!" If we do this, and continually wash ourselves from our sins in Holy Confession, the Saviour will continually bestow His grace upon us, He will grant us the gift of His Most Holy Spirit and our spiritual blindness will be healed.

They brought him who formerly was blind to the Pharisees. Now it was a Sabbath when Jesus made the clay and opened his eyes. Then the Pharisees also asked him again how he had received his sight. He said to them, "He put clay on my eyes, and I washed, and I see." Therefore some of the Pharisees said, "This Man is not from God, because He does not keep the Sabbath." (John 9: 13-16 NKJV)

Fr Ted Bobosh of the Eastern Orthodox Church suggests that this verse denotes a different kind of blindness, willing blindness. The man describes an act of God – taking clay and creating eyes that had never worked before. This is not restoring sight to the blind, but giving him sight for the first time. The Pharisees can't see God in this at all. The only thing they can see is a violation of their understanding of Torah. They are blind to what the healing might represent, and declare first, before any further investigation, that this is not from God. They are not willing to see what might be true and choose not to see what is in front of their eyes. It is not that it would be impossible for them to see it, they instead decide not to see it.

How many times in our lives have we overlooked God's hand and failed to credit Him? Look back at the last years of your life, there have surely been times where you have felt helpless. These are the times where Christ has supported you most.

In order to ensure that after receiving the healing of Christ we do not become like the Pharisees, we must follow the instructions of St. Paul in Colossians 3:17:

And whatever you do in word or deed, do all in the name of the Lord Jesus, giving thanks to God the Father through Him.

What does it mean to do something "in the name of" someone? If I'm going to do something "in the name of Xavier's School" (where I go to school), I am going to be representing my school in what I do. This is often why teachers can be so strict about the way you present yourself and behave when in school uniform! Whether I mean it or not, every time I wear that uniform I am acting as a representative of the school, meaning that this is how those who go to my school would behave. I could reflect well on the school or reflect badly.

In the same way as Christians, everything we do reflects how we view God. If we live for God's glory, we live in a way that makes God look glorious. We're going to obey Him and make His law something attractive to follow for all who see us. In that way, we acknowledge Him and His presence in our lives.

What the Fathers Say

"But it was no disadvantage to be put out the synagogue since the one they cast out, Christ received"

– St. Augustine

FOOTPRINTS IN THE SAND

One night I dreamed a dream.

As I was walking along the beach with my Lord.

Across the dark sky flashed scenes from my life.

For each scene, I noticed two sets of footprints in the sand,

One belonging to me and one to my Lord.

After the last scene of my life flashed before me,

I looked back at the footprints in the sand.

I noticed that at many times along the path of my life,

especially at the very lowest and saddest times,

there was only one set of footprints.

This really troubled me, so I asked the Lord about it.

"Lord, you said once I decided to follow you,

You'd walk with me all the way.

But I noticed that during the saddest and most troublesome times of my life,

there was only one set of footprints.

I don't understand why, when I needed You the most, You would leave me."

He whispered, "My precious child, I love you and will never leave you

Never, ever, during your trials and testings.

When you saw only one set of footprints,

It was then that I carried you."

HOLY WEEK PREP

PREPARATION FOR HOLY WEEK & CONCLUSION

Although it may seem that the journey of Lent has now ended, it is only just beginning as the most significant week of the Fast approaches followed by the fifty days of glory and joy of the Ressurection period as Christ grants us salvation through His Holy Resurrection. Channelling all your effort into the coming week and trying to make it into a lifestyle will be a difficult task at first but the rewards for your spiritual life are truly life changing as you come closer in unity with God.

The Coptic Orthodox Diocese of Los Angeles under the blessing of His Grace Bishop Serapion has compiled a series of guidelines to remember when preparing for Holy week and partaking in the Holy Pascha.

1. Our Behavior Inside and Outside of Church

It is very noticeable that many people during Pascha Week are one thing inside church and completely different outside. Inside church, black curtains, somber hymns, solemn readings, and concentrating on the suffering of Christ. Outside of church, we often laugh, joke around, socialise, think and talk about many worldly issues. We lose all the spiritual depth that we gained inside church. Let us concentrate our thoughts, conversations, and meditations around the events of this Holy Week and the Passion of our Saviour.

2. Retreat

During our regular fasting days, we put the words of the bible before us - "Consecrate a fast, call a sacred assembly" (Joel 1:14). How much more then should we apply this commandment during Holy Week? This week should be characterised by solitude and retreat with God, by staying away from meaningless discussions and various means of entertainment or pleasure. Reserve your time for God and spiritual activities worthy of this week. That means this week you should give up social media, technology and TV, instead focusing on spiritually beneficial activities.

In the first hour of the Monday of the Holy Pascha, we read St. Shenouda's homily, which warns us: "Brethren if we want to escape

God's punishment and find mercy in His eyes, let us sit every evening alone by ourselves and search our souls...

3. Follow the Steps of Christ

Meditate on the events of the week one by one: from Palm Sunday, when Christ refused His worldly kingdom and the Jews gave up their hope in Him, until they crucified and buried Him. On Palm Sunday, ask yourself, "Is Christ King and Lord over everything in my life? Do I, like Christ, turn down worldly glory for spiritual and eternal glory? During the General Funeral Service, do I consider myself attending my own funeral?"

And when the church denounces Judas' traitorous kiss on the eve of the Wednesday of Pascha Week, ask yourself in prayer, "How often, O Lord have I betrayed You? How many times have I told You words of love in prayers, while my actions show the opposite and my heart is far away from You?"

Try to apply this principle for every event that happens this week.

4. Share in the Fellowship of His Suffering

Saint Paul said, "That I may know Him and the power of His resurrection, and the fellowship of His suffering, being conformed to His death." (Philippians 3:10) Can we give ourselves an exercise this week to share in the fellowship of His suffering and be conformed to His death? Can we follow Him in His suffering and ascend with Him to the Cross? Can we say with St. Paul, "With Christ I have been crucified; it is no longer I who live, but Christ who lives in me." (Galatians 2:20).

Therefore, in order for Christ to live in us, we have to carry our cross and follow Him. If you have a cross in your life, do not complain about it. Instead, rejoice in it and bear it for Christ's sake - "for to you has been granted on behalf of Christ, not only to believe in Him but to suffer for His sake." (Philippians 1:29).

5. Asceticism

Whoever puts the suffering of Christ before him will not take any pleasure in eating and drinking or pampering the body. But in order to succeed in pursuing asceticism, we must satisfy our souls with spiritual food so that it may thrive and overcome physical hunger. It was customary for the Church to fast until at least the 9th hour on normal fasting days and until sunset during the Holy Week of Pascha.

St. Athanasius even declared that this period of Holy Week should be received with "longer prayers, fasts, and vigils so that we may be able to anoint our lintels with precious blood and escape the destroyer." And again, the blessed saint says, "Let us thus engage in the holy fasts, as having been prescribed by Him, and by means of which we find the way to God."

So, this Holy week, make it a habit to fast as long as you can in the day without any food or water, at the very minimum until after the morning Pascha.

6. Spiritual Readings

Spiritual readings are also food for the soul. The church has organised for us a treasure of appropriate readings for every day of the Holy Week comprised of Gospel readings; Old Testament prophesies that correspond to the events of each day, spiritual explanations and sermons of the Church Fathers. On Bright Saturday (Apocalypse night) the church reads the entire Book of Revelation.

In this week, aside from reading along in the services, it is important that you fill your mind with other spiritual books including commentaries on the Gospels, contemplations, stories of the Fathers and, of course, the Bible.

7. Hymns

The hymns of the Pascha Week are moving and full of spiritual depth. Hymns, like reading, preserve the thought from wandering and guide it in spiritual direction. We should continue to recite the hymns while walking, meditating and resting.

8. Prayer

Since the prayers of the Agpeya are not used during Holy Week, we are to substitute personal prayers in their place. In addition to the intensive prayers of the church we should ask the Lord who bore the sins of the world and died for us to forgive and have mercy upon us according to His great mercy.

9. Confession and Communion

During this week, each person must sit with himself and remember his sins and put them on Christ's shoulders and tell Him in shame, "Carry O Lord my sins too, with the sins of the rest of humanity. Take my sins and nail them to the Cross with You, so that Your Blood may wipe them away!"

Look carefully at your sins and know that they are the cause of His crucifixion. Many people cry out of their sorrow for Christ's suffering while they crucify Him every day with their sins. We should not feel sorry for Christ during this week, but should be sorry for our sins that caused Him these pains. As Jesus told the women that were crying over Him, "Daughters of Jerusalem, do not cry for Me, but cry for yourselves and your children." (Luke 23:28).

Before the Cross, we all stand as sinners, all under the condemnation. "no one is righteous, not even one." (Psalm 14:3). We confess our sins and prepare ourselves for communion. There are three liturgies one should attend during Holy Week: on Passover Thursday, Holy Saturday, and Easter Sunday (preceded, of course, by the Liturgy of Palm Sunday).

10. Spiritual Storage

Pascha Week is not an opportunity to benefit for a week only, but a time to store up spiritual nourishment enough to last the whole year, particularly needed during the 50 days after the Resurrection when there is no fasting.

Taking all these things into consideration having spent the Lent period in fasting and prayer will be the most beneficial way to reap maximum benefit from this blessed period. Remember that your journey to Christ is only just beginning and that if taken seriously it is a lifelong path filled with great joy and comfort until Christ raises us with Him to Heaven.

Over the Pascha week period there is another book in this series entitled "Holy Week For Teens" which would be highly recommended in helping you understand the events and significance of each day.

Lightning Source UK Ltd.
Milton Keynes UK
UKHW041113171122
412294UK00021B/22